OSSEIN

Joseph D. Brutto

DEDICATION

Dedicated to my biggest advocate, my literal savior, to a paragon of
humanity, the catalyst for all that has happened in the last six years, this
is all dedicated to the person I could cry to when I couldn't hold it in any
longer, to the person who always believed in me, this book of poetry is
dedicated to my Mother.

ACKNOWLEDGMENTS

First I have to thank my Mother for supporting me all my life as I wouldn't be where I am without her, I also thank Jeff Mach for taking a chance with a sixteen-year old poet to read at his conventions where I got a chance for invaluable experience. I thank my teachers Kim Henderson and Alice Bolin for what they've taught me and for putting in the time as well for one on one sessions helping me revise my work.

An angel rests upon the shoulder or as you'd call it, a fairy, as they'd call it my conscious but why is my conscious your conscious? Strange, I thought you'd notice that. It's influencing you to feed that bird, play with that puppy, stab your mother, catch that balloon, and give to charity.

A BOY WHO DRESSES LIKE A GIRL. . .

She holds this gun under her chin

He's cradling it like a child

The heated steel leaves his skin, her makeup, his identity lost in the bullet's flame

For so long she had been surviving

But every moment they met, everyone destroyed him and stripped her from his personality's hold

Everyone screamed, just die!

Just... just fucking die!

He tried to escape

But each time she was dragged back again

Pushed 10 feet down under the school's athletic pool

The cloudy unfiltered water dripping from his skin leaving it so cold, yet so softened

All the sick tasting chlorine poured into his lungs

As he tried keeping her dry, keeping her hair together, her eyeliner un-smudged, her dress in one piece

But the mass liquid engulfed them

Every single thing was falling apart before his very eyes

It left him feeling so molested, her so broken

He couldn't stop reimagining the nightmares from when he was that innocent small boy

Hours pass as he's drowned and dunked

His heart pruned from the waters, his skin torn from the finger nails scratching her keeping them under

He's crawling back to solid ground, panting from the hours of torture

And though all the soaking water is running from his pores, his heart still has flame

It still has that audacity, her heart is still burning with this stupid fucking audacity

It's still burning. . .

Just like the cold fire that coats their hometown

That coats their crosses

That coats their pictures together

That cold fire burning

His mind is spiraling

Everything he imagines is pure dysphoria tearing at his mind

Bleeding it slow

Every time he dreams of putting on that dress

She flashes back to him watching her being skinned in front of him

Skinned down to her origins

But he crawls on, unwillingly continuing to be himself

His eyes lose focus, her vison softens

Everything he stares at is fading

But there she stood, looking down upon him

Her blood dripping, diffusing into the pool water

Her nose bloody, her fists - her forearms so beaten and bruised

So pained

But like him, she's still alive she still has that rebellious look

They pick themselves up, but why don't they understand. . .

Each time they're so fucking miserable

By the preacher's hand they're beaten with the bible

He has to be punished. . .

The toxic scented candles flow across the church's narrow decorated halls

The stench streams through just like his screams, her screams

It shatters the holy peace

The fragile silence cracks away and dies

Like his sanity, but as the whips snap at his flesh his screams soften

"What a Sadomasochist" the preacher remarks. His perverted smile widens

Enduring the molestation, her mind goes numb

His body inert with pain

Why?

This sexual ache, this sexual desire, has him in sinful tears

As these holy men keep him tormented

His body no longer feels.

The scars and calluses numb the skin

Is she finally dead?...

His identity has conformed

Bruises that cover him

Soften the skin

Like a dying fruit from God's tree

Freezing his life into a prison cell

The dress on the other side

He cries as he watches them stain it... burn it

His shoulders banging against the bars, trying to reach for her

It's too late, she's been burnt to dust

He's panicking, crying, grabbing at the remnants of his dress

Tears flood out

The same tears that have mixed in with the blood

Everything around him fades to ash

He's alone again,

No one to hold onto,

No one to run to,

Just like when he was a child...

But back then he had a reason to continue, to become what he is today

Now he has nothing to keep him sane, nothing to keep him free

Nothing for him to live for

He wants to do what everything he loved did, he wants to die

But he can't seem to gather the last bits of strength to hold up the gun, he writhes

Curling up, nervously sweating

He can't refrain

He can't stop imagining her

Her dressed in that flame

For when he was she, the world felt free, he felt free

Child to Teen to this strange example of a Man,

A man cursed to be tormented

Grabbing at his hairs, shutting his eyes

He can't escape those still images of his dress

Die they said, just fucking die

So he did

The loud steel churning through the flesh and bone

It echoes through the neighborhood

As his body plummeted to the floor

And for a mere second the world flooded instantly

Like that of the athletic pool

There in that unreal posthumous experience, he witnessed her cold body floating across the waters

Blood fusing with the filtered liquid, melting out from her head

Then suddenly the world around him softened

Joseph D. Brutto

CONCUPISCENT SIN UNDER VIRGIN GRACE

You and I
Dispersing across a sea of souls
No longer able to feel
The numb vibrations of Death's orchestra
The violins that attune with our heartbeats
Plummeting and devouring the statuettes of kings
Priests
And clergy men
A noble fund
Of blood and devotion
Is for not
The rotting sensations this warm air produces
Born from a decrepit tree
That lays in this field of ash
Smoldering faces stare out into our innocence
Only to consume us as a whole
We depart this bottle of black sand
Instead deluging our young
Into a lake of blood and bone
Remnants of white blood cells levitate forth
You faded as their nucleus unifies into my child
Each section patches together like broken porcelain
Stained with sin
Original sin
I pull on Grandmother's opera gloves
Soaking with grime
And I adorn this garb of bone and a thousand feathers of dove
The strumming of my ethereal harp
Soothes the creature
The menial movements stop its pulse
I fall back, diverged from my original plane
My realm of irregular pretense
I lay upon a vanilla fern
Vibrant pollen, tinted maroon, floats above me
Sending each to heaven
A cello illuminates the divine realm
With a maudlin ballet
Dark strokes deepen their pitch
As this unholy string is pulled
It utters a shrill cry
As the pinpoints lengthen out
And you arise
You changed

The piano pulls you in, your fingers pushing down into the vellum
textured keys
Each time dulling the skin
I sit and listen
Focused on your randomized sounds
I'm poured a glass of God's liquid breath
And we watch your chastity closely
Black rabbits run from the fatal push of the keys
My lips stain red from this sacrilegious wine
As our minds blend with our blood
You scream
You've broken my seal
My oath
You've killed the virgin lamb
And now there's just me
The supple pain brands your bosom
And I have spilt my wine
As I have spilt your blood
The abuse turns to mutilation
Mutilation of the womb
And the strumming goes still
As I transfer my folly
A faint exposer of my defiled anatomy
It's swallowing the lead that coursed through your feeble body
And here we tremble
Defunct under the rain

Joseph D. Brutto

WEIRD DAYS

I woke up today
With a nosebleed

I don't get those too often
My hair fell out
I glued it all back in

And with that my day started
A warm chill pushed me into it all

Right into God's mercy
Right under Big Bertha
Her mass crushed me with a child of death

Heavy drugs
And cement

"Dun, Dun, Dun, Duhna, Tah, Tah, Taha
Bum, Dun, Dunnah, Duhn, Duhn, Duhna"
My music box concurred

I woke up tomorrow
With blood in my sheets today
Your sounds pulling me out of bed

I found you there,
strumming a broken string

So I sat on the bathroom floor
I drummed with my fingers on the wall
You stared and smiled as I followed along

I couldn't help but smile too
And with that my day started

I woke up yesterday
In the middle of the forest
It was strange, cold; I hadn't worn anything to bed

Not the night before
But the night before that

So I gathered deteriorated crayons and I broke the trees

OSSEIN

Since they leaned over to see what I was drawing
I wouldn't show them. . . So they bent. . .

And they bent. . . Until
They all cracked in half

And with that my day started
With a splinter in my pinky toe
And lady bugs crawling on my arms

I woke up tomorrow night
With lost breath

I saw you there too, playing another broken cord
And there was a noose holding me up
Myself pretending to fly

A gurney and machines
Pumps and an eerie slow panic
The golden sunlight and a rose covered casket

I can't really explain it
But I can't seem to wake up again. . .

And with that my day started

MISCREATION

After each scream that cracks my voice
After each bloody beating that brands my mentality with scars
After each drop of sweat mixes with every escaping tear
that follows the staining stream
of blood flooding from my body
I seem to go blind
As my pupils burst
and leak across
my charcoal covered cheeks
I solemnly peel off my bruised skin like a mask
Slowly ripping out bundles of my broken hair
Chunk by chunk I'm tearing away sorrows of the past
I dig my dirty bloody nails into my exposed body
Breaking every tendon and muscle that's stuck to my bone
I rip off my jaw as I pull out my slimy damaged tongue,
it slowly slides out across the floor
Alone, falling apart, tremors echo through
Shattering the cortex of my brain
It seems to be shot
I'm staring at the remains of what used to be me
Now I'm an advent,
a mute husk drawing in its
own fucking blood & misery
and acclaiming it as "Poetry"

BIOMECHANICAL MUTILATION

Cold, deteriorated
His flesh drips
Chunks sliding between his feet
His skull breaking apart
Suddenly the ground is entranced
The rocks, the dead yellow grass, the piss stained walls
They reverberate in collapsing recession
With the percussion of Earth
He feels his body slowly crawl back into itself
Skull fitting into its place, inner locking with the marrow
Jolting in between each electron
Infusing together with each molecule
The blood tinted steam bursting from the rusty recalibration
It diffuses into the room, the morbid smell
That smell of toxic steel quality skin switching their cells back and forth
Eyes, with their galactic gleaming rings, gravitate towards the naked pupil
It's trying to focus on the image reflecting off its sleek organic screen
His chest, with the ribs stabbing outwards like a rose in blossom, pulses
Purging the nuts and bolts and the fuel that trickles down, pooling in his belly button
The cogs riming his heart struggle, they seem to be stuck in hiatus for everything's coming loose
The rotating bronze cracks inside, energetically reengineering the copper cartilage
As the torn holes and bloodless strips opening wider in his forearm try to enclose
Engaging in an electric prism meticulously piecing together every inch of the synthetic skins
This automatic apparatus trimming each section to an exact clicks and clacks across the muscles
As the torn tissue hangs against the automation goose-bumps
Across his hands lay this implemented hardware
This silicon installation moving each bone, each finger that becomes a new contraption
Clamps quickly piercing through falling gore, shaking, stained crimson, still holding it in place
A network webbing through his veins, coating the inside with titanium tubes
Imploding into a star, formed from metallic mackintosh
The CPU is placing his heart in recrudescence
His lungs, meshed in a gleaming chromium alloy

Filtering new refreshing oxygen through his body
His iron anthracite spine contracts as he begins to move again
The reflection in his silver bones shines incandescently
His mind, cycling it's pipes and cogs for an electric pulse it can't seem to answer
Its mechanical thoughts are as empty as the soul under that steel, he's in a quandary
But nothing can seem to repair this error in the stem of his motherboard
The cords stretching through his scalp, wrap across his bones and silver veins
They dig through his feeble flesh and connect
The adapters poke through his loose skin like broken bones
Has he been patched?
Protected in his wall of steel
His shell of silver
His prison of proxy servers
His aegis of aluminum
His farrago of foreign matter…

I JUST WANTED TO SAY HI, I JUST WANTED TO SAY GOODBYE

A vanilla cream melting down, fusing into this urn filled with Frankin
A chrome fixture swaying left to right breaking the vibrations of your
hollow voice
Swift actions passing quickly by my body
What do I do?
Just cooking under this rock
Awaiting his return
He's going to lift this stone, he's going to sit with me in my own world
He's going to rip away the separations of an untimely end so we can
finally meet
But he's not coming back. . .
His necklace sways in these dark warm winds
A supple embrace clinging to a hope
Clinging to a prayer in the night
I just want to say goodbye, but there seems to be no God to pass it on
His essence is still perfectly untouched, still soaking with fidelity
Silly faces reflect in the decadent puddles of this new world
A reborn Earth, no longer the Heaven it used to be
It has lost its last angel
2013th year
and December was the coldest it's ever been
It's felt a little bit colder ever since
I just wanted to say Hi, but there seems to be no heartbeat to understand
I thought moving on would be easy
But the transition seems impossible
The weight of the unamendable pain weighs us all down
And this warm wind keeps getting colder
You're in so many of my poems you know, no one really noticed

It's been a year
And each passing day I feel like I'm getting closer
Closer to saying Hello
Sometimes I talk to you, but I know you aren't really there
My friends thought I was crazy speaking to desolate air
2014th year
And I still look to the stars, I still practice what I'll say when I meet you up
there. . .

ANGEL

Violently as each breath is tugged out from his lungs
The ropes tied at each end, drenched in sorrow and crimson stains of blood
The spiders gorging on each bit of his tattered tainted body, dehumanizing him
Tearing away his skin, his conviction, his morality and sin..
Tearing away his humanity as those spiders stuff themselves with chunks of his fragile dying limbs
The burning beating heart inside his soft decaying flesh is about to give in
For the knives and hooks that have slithered into his back are forged from the toxic arrays of hatred that already paint his torn shredded skin
The blades poison his soul with stress as his mind submits to peer pressures and every screaming wish that society's norm has been cramming into his mind, the same wishes he clenches in his fists
The wishes he cannot seem to break, even though according to society he's the monster with inhuman strength
But to many he was the angel that society wasn't ready for, the misunderstood angel
He couldn't carry on with the weight of insults and relentless hatred
So he escaped
Like many before him
because he's only human
and yet still they haunt him in death
Behind keyboards are the bullies
That made the angel someone I'll never forget

Phantasmagoria, The Lost Recant, Scripture Of Memories Dread

It's grieving, fingers twitching back and forth
Severed fingers and some sick morning resurrection
They still seem so alive, there is a pulse you know but it all lacks a heart
Their cells stitch into the influx of materialized data
The horde of aluminum tears chokes it up
It grows a throat, a tongue, to swallow this pain
This ethereal fear of the irreversible touch of death
The bones that pierce the image with horror crawl into it's mechanical
embrace
Gears that crack into themselves quicken, the teeth of this mechanism
This dying machine has begun to crawl, eerie in it's movement
The darkness that surrounds it is fitting to it's freakish look
It's an arousing miscreation, a birthplace to fear
The lack of light leaves it misguided so it chokes down a flame
A malady of burning fire that laid within human hearts
It found this cold burlesque, soggy and barely beating soul within a
puddle
It was veiled over by a torn soaking wet dress
But through the second skin of stitching it glowed
These aluminum sinews pull it within, so it can be warm, so it can serve
its purpose
This monstrosity of metal has qualities of our being
The strange thing, born of twilight and ecclesiastical hatred, squirms
through these dark caves
It's light shows the lonely umbra of truth to where all these things
slumber in wait
It moves in feeble broken circles; its lost
Until he came along, he picked up this embodiment of infidelity, this
frightening thing
His lukewarm touch seemed to increase the beat of that stolen heart
The light inside grew incandescent compared to the dim flame of before
He used it as a guiding light, through these dark caves
He used the monster as a tool to see through what you could not
For once it had a purpose, a penance
A purpose
A penance
A purpose
Does it not compute?

It fell with its capture, it became a broken lantern
yet it seems more fixed, updated, more purposeful than ever
It cast light into that innocent, that weak
That boy lost in the dark

WHERE ARE YOU GOING?

I loved you yet I was the vein of your pleasure, nothing more.

I gave you my heart, and you bled it over me. Once I dried, I became the scab across your skin... Unwanted. You left me on the pavement without a second thought as I watched you walk away. My life wasn't real without your false love.

My crimson tears ran down my face as I got up only to see your shadow fade then suddenly the world enclosed on me, my lungs empty, my heart non-existent as my body began to shut down from its loss.

My skin dried out, bound to my skeleton, my flesh, there was none, my hair, gray as the clouds near the moon, my bones, feeble and hollow. Suddenly, I hit the floor with only eyes and ossein remaining, my body broke away like sand in the desert wind and my last visions were of you leaving me to die after you used me up to only your gain.

My life was over in just a moment, my soul drifting to the stars.

My judgment was soon to come as my ghostly tears dripped like a broken faucet
The city began to rain and fog, but I forgive you somehow. I forgive you even after all that's happened. And in a few days, I will be forgotten, just another victim of love's poisonous bite.

THE ANGUISHED WRITER

Seventeen strokes of a pen

Across his forehead

The ink seeps in

Burning across the weakened skin

It melts down into his eyes

Yet he can see clearer than before

But blinded by ink blots smudged across soaked paper hearts

The texture like the feet of bugs

It trickles out onto the sheets on which he writes

His bleak, black eyes, wide, focused

As his hand rips in with the pen

The papers, thrown away, crawl up his back

Paper limb after paper limb penetrate deep

Piercing his lungs

Cringing him back

Void of air

The papers wrap across his mouth and clog into his trachea

Then across his eyes, pulling them from the sockets

And finally, deep within his ears, popping the drums

His realities are ink strokes

He is now deaf to society and consumed by imagination

DETRIMENTAL

My skin doesn't seem to fit
It strangles my soul
My bones crack from this ever growing mass of pressure
And as I see a bleak future full of failure
My hope turns to ash and floods my lungs
But instead of smoke I cough out dirt and earth
For my self-conscious fears are spoon feeding me this awful ground
I'm eating a grave
Suddenly a bullet storm of regrets pierces through my body and pushes
me into the dark hole I've eaten
A veil covers me and through the linen I see the silhouettes of everyone
who's screams of anger is directed at me
The yells and swears ravage my soul, they materialize into needles and
pins, each poking through this blinding fabric
And suddenly that pressure intensifies and pushes the needle infested
fabric down into me..
I try to scream but I'm muffled by dirt crammed down my throat, a flower
grows out of my mouth
And now as every metal pin paralyzes my muscles
I can feel a meat hook slide through my eye and out my skull
Suddenly it raises me, covered by a silky veil and paralyzed
I can see obsidian tendrils crawl from my heart that seems to be opened,
stained black with ink and covered in stitches
Those tendrils paint the walls of this imaginary realm I can see
Rain begins to pour as a cold desolate wind sways the meat hook's rope
and it seems to break
I fall
Stained with mud and ink
But I walk and wander this distorted plane of my imagination
The plants appear dead as their flowers break apart from the wind's gust
the trees are grey, the pitch black leaves fly off and melt to sand
I feel the storm in my brain pick up and suddenly the screams of the past
crawl across my toes, their claws innocently stab through my already
torn skin
I fall through the floor and there I feel the beat
The beat of the hammers sealing all my friend's fate
Their coffins crumble through the dirt and out rises fly's eating away the
tips of my fingers, they're the remnants I can't seem to forget, the

unwanted knowledge of how my hands are stained with their blood
I can feel that noose, the rotten noose
Comprised of misery
It seems to be what's in style these days

THE PURGE OF WORDS

Purged cathartically through this conversion of blood to ink
And though the skin on my lips merge together, muffling my voice, I still
seem to speak a thousand words
Emotionally struck as every silent scream revamps the self-expression
Revamps the toxic effect of every droplet of ink dripping from this rusty
syringe people call poetry
Revamps the complexity of the clockwork puzzle in my head.. Oh the
confusing fucking clockwork puzzle in my head
The one that seems to rim the bumps and ragged jags of my brain and
the veins that're bursting full of insecurity and madness
The one that locks me away, leaving me alone in what feels like a prison
where every single unwanted thought echoes back to me
Is this the damned thing what will bring me fame and acknowledgement?
Will this revelation that seems to claw into my fears and secrets then
finger paint them across a canvas of big words and fucked up images be
the one thing that will bring forth reality to my dreams?..
I begin vomiting each word I read
Every syllable is like a pin through my twitching tongue
As I struggle to simply hold up this accursed sheet coated with my
broken sanity and my screams of sorrow..

ASPHYXIATION IN THE STREET-ALLEY'S VOID

Gurgling on a materialized scripture
Comprised of decayed lung tissue
She picks at her body's scabs
Hampering the skin's process
Agitating the womb's eye
of flesh and false pretense

It's gaze imbuing her mind with suicide
and a detaching plea to reality
A faint trace of posthumous steam sprouts
Cracking through the illustrious marrow

It's smoke lays the options to rest
Under a thick organic jacket
Stitched together with the sinner's milk
The retinal artery severs
painting the pupil crimson
As the sleeves tie, restraining resistance
Futile resistance

The needle culminates under the system's filth
The unfeigned fear is embodying the soul
Squeezing out noisome excrement
As this cloud's toxic umbra veils forth
Argon filling the mouths of innocents
Hunched over, choking on her customer
Disgusting
It's all just to satisfy needs

Now footsteps melt into the floor
The floor that resonates all this wasted potential
With the sound of high heels to alley cement
"Let the child speak"
"Let the child think"
Just for once

Smeared lipstick melting from the heat's ash
The cherry drops
As the raincloud of cigarette smoke and arsenic pool
Giving birth to the crooked halo over her head

Raining down regrets and premature aging
Premature maternity
Premature everything

The thigh cracks
As her knees trickle mud
Her callused fingertips pressed against the framework
The rusted framework that displays a polaroid
Honey tinted pigtails and that stupid looking dress
A bolus of red dripping into the cracks of Earth
A lighter's flame under remnants of memory
Under purity in its purest form
It's most ignorant form
Childhood

Pulsing the reflecting information
Lynching it between the iris
Rimmed by broken veins
Broken windows to the soul
Hot sweat follows the pore
Oozing through makeup
Like the preverbal tears diffusing across a sun-kissed face

Yesterday
Today
The grim truth shines on both
They'll never not be the same

THE BROKEN MASK

Covered by a masquerade mask

The screams vibrate through its porcelain shell

The ever growing shudder of the underwhelming truth

Cracking away at the beauty of the broken mask

Just as it is stripped away

The hell that they conjured pulls me down

Inch by inch

My feet are buried in flames

The normal embrace of these tortures slice into my being

They stare at what lays skin deep, at what flourishes off the blood and leaking cries

The plague is inside

Every bacteria is simply born from cultural viruses

Diseases

Exposed

I simply degrade

WHO AM I NOW?

After each scream that cracks my voice
After each bloody beating that brands my flesh with scars
After each drop of sweat is mixed with every one of my following tears
Each seem to slide in with the staining stream of blood oozing from my body
I seem to go blind
My pupils bursting and leaking across my eyes
I solemnly peel off my bruised skin like a mask
Slowly rip out bundles of my broken hair
Chunk by chunk I tear away sorrows of the past
I dig my dirty bloody nails into my exposed flesh
Tearing every tissue and muscle that's sticking to my bone
All these blood ridden tears running down the flesh and melting across the naked joints
I rip away my jaw as I pull out my slimy tongue, it slowly slides out onto the floor
Alone, falling apart, my mind seems to be shot
I'm staring at the remains of what used to be who I was
Now I'm a monster, a mute husk drawing in its own fucking blood & tears and calling it "Poetry"

IMMURATION

Featherless ravens are flapping their boney wings
As the chains of devotion scratch across the ever dark prison called love
The moans of disgust echo through the subliminal halls
Whilst the milk white skin of my lifeless body crawls
Slowly the rusty chains bind against my motionless limbs
Bound down by "love"
While the chemical reaction is softly pumped through the fragile veins of this dead body of mine
My arms begin to twitch as I vomit out my heart
As I lay there these heavy breaths echo
The blood in my system no longer circulates
The poisons of love are no more
As I begin to tear each chain from my forearms and thighs
Suddenly I grade my scabbed finger tips against the concrete walls of this hypothetical asylum
Each shadow of every so called lover begins to pull me away
Inch by inch I am dragged by each memory
Forming new chains, my recollections pulsate those familiar pains
This omission is grinding up my will
For every time I try to escape, these memorial remnants chase me
Hunt me like the monstrosity I am
A social monstrosity
The chains are again nestled against my body
The memories are crippling
Whisper after whisper crawl into my ears
They begin to shout revelations that melt through my skull and awake my mind
Oh the taste of my blood flooding my mouth is refreshing
For it shows I'm still alive
Chain after chain break apart
The sounds of metal against floor are the anthem to this rise
Flames of the phoenix burn away the slurs piercing my revival
This prison that I've subliminally locked myself away in is crumbling
The cuffs are fading into ash
As the tears that wash away the blood evaporate
My anatomy has been patched
But abysmal screams push me back

The muscle and tendons under my skin have regrown
Whilst they take the encumbering shock of each insult yelled
And as the spit from those screams smashes against my skin
The ones who've helped rebuild the cells in it turn to dust in time
The intensity begins to put out the flame of revolt
Only a dull ember remains
As ink drips out from my eyes in place of tears
Blinding me but also expressing each scream into a calm sentence
If you listen closely you'll hear each tendon rip
as the skin in my feet is tearing off
"let it out"
"let it out"
They scream
Then suddenly there is silence
for it seems I've broken free
yet I can see the featherless ravens mocking at me
Squawking at my insolence
Laughing at my ignorance
They fall upon their saggy featherless backs chortling at my idiocy

CONGESTIVE HEART FAILURE

My obsidian eyes pulse
Reflecting the nightmares that have been burnt across the iris
The holy men and children decorating one section in the screaming
words of "Harlot" and "Heretic" as they both scratch into my skin in the
decor of crimson blood
and burgundy scars
My fear imbued iris rotates itself, stopping like a jammed cog, but instead
of dusk and sprockets it spews out blood & diseased flesh
It now displays the endless nights of confusion and self-judgment, I
couldn't stop asking why am I such a defiled innocent, why am I a lost
soul caught in this
so-called web of Beelzebub and other malicious figures, why are the
people I love a Sin that's marking me
Crying out to the loving father I never had, the only father I could love
back, crying to normal, to be free of the darkness I've prescribed myself
deep inside
But all he presented me were demons dressed in the skin of men
The color of my eye's is from the shit that has been shoved in them, its
mud and dirt and squashed bugs from the boots that have stomped on
my skull, and stirred in
is the brown decay of decomposition
My eyes begin leaking the black within my pupils, its ink inside them and
the flowing shine that gleams off follows the ridged paths of pulsing veins
Inevitably running across my cold, eaten face
My iris turns once again, pushing out puss, blood and small insects
frightened from the motion
Now come close, the image laying within is shadowy, it is hard to see but
it is there.. Not many were able to view this, so look close.. please,
please look fucking harder
Closer!
Closeeer!!
My lungs flail in pumps as I scream to you
My heart pulses faster and faster, the stiches inside it are bursting at the
blood stained seams
Could you see the depressions, the sadness, the insatiable self-
indulgence, the secret hatreds that are slowly diseasing through the
cords of my eyes with
black electricity, dark embryotic pathogens, born from hatred, pure
hatred that has been born out of the seclusion the fucking seclusion, the
hypothetical white boxes
I've been stuck in are painted sanguine and I've been duct-taped
together, breaking apart but still all my pieces are forged together
The feet of roaches are suddenly crawling across the cracked glass of

my eyes
If these are the windows to the soul then what does my soul look like
The therapists asked that, not the same way but never the less they
asked that
So they tried cleaning out my dirty rotten stomach, my veins, my acidic
heart with malformed pills
And that, with a little bit of prayer, brought my purity back
But like this emotional Frankenstein I am, I turned on the one who
resurrected me
The cortex inside my mind flinched and trembled as the purity pruned
into a whore, a Satanic slut among Holy men, a bloody serrated smile
compared with a set
of pearly whites, I'm a ugly decayed dead boy dancing with the beautiful
perfect living
I'm so inured with this unnatural darkness that I don't understand
holiness, kindness, humanity anymore
I used to praise our loving God now I curse his name
I'd ask God to save me a place in Hell, I'd scream to him in the rain how
mad he's made me, how cursed his little angel has become, how far his
angel spiraled down
but he never cared, for I'm already in Hell, a beautifully disgusting Hell

EFFECTS

Tears melting into cheeks
Sanity breaking away from mind
Eyes blood shot, yet shine so divine
Lips quivering as fingers pierce the dirt
Broken mud stains the skin as finger nails bleed
Teeth grinding, cracking each time
Voice breaking, denying... Facts of the future
Muscles tense strained from the pressure
Screaming at the moon, yelling... Till' neighbors call the police
Suicide develops as butterflies float by
Is this a nightmare or a dark false reality?
45' pointed over closed eyes
Lead won't wake you up child

CHERUB'S DECENT

Crawling from the kingdom of luminous gold, dripping materialized sin
from my bellybutton
My wings flail through the chilled blessed wind
The decaying pulpit in which I lay upon crackles, swaying from my weight
Burlesque masters laugh, coughing on their tongues, as the skin
wrapping across my luscious feathers breaks off
This dark malady of sin is altering who I am
I finally fall
The exceeding wind resistance tears away any holy remnant
Breaking my wings
Dissolving my halo
Their mirth haunting me as my decent quickens
I hit the muddy earth like a comet streaming across the twilight's dulling
glow
An ember, in dirty bloody snow, sinking through the steaming crater
I rise
As bloodied tears pool across my bent lashes
My muscles tremble, broken, my body gives into the mortal pain
I curl up
Revolving in the sticky heated mud and tar
My stimulus was the sacrilegious darkness I was born with
Irredeemably cursed
I wander the plains of this ancient hell I've found myself lost in
Naked and stripped, cold and inhuman, fallen and barely alive
Under the mercy of mere man
The eternally bleeding wounds of my denuded wings trickle across the
crumbling ground, leaving my apoplectic mind deprived of its
nourishment; it's well deserved blood
Stumbling throughout the white snow sheeted forests I lightly faint
forward
My alabaster skin blends me in, hiding my feeble flesh from
malnourished hellhounds and bloodthirsty witch hunters
As I softly sleep in a freezing spread of frost I grab at my skull
My temples
The enormous pain is impossible to bare
I'm on my scrapped knees screaming for repentance, acceptance
Mercy...
But my grasp instead holds onto a product of evil
A symbolic forgery of sin breaking through my skull, stretching my skin
outwards until it finally rips through
The horns are growing...
I crawl to a nearby tree, shoving my fingers into the cold ice ridden bark
My tight grasp breaks through its thick crystallized stem
The warm crimson running from my pierced palms thaws my broken bits

of flesh
But when I look into my wounds it's not red, it's jet-black
The dark tint of crushed blueberries
And my blood is no pastel sanguine
For its ink black and thicker than the snow falling against my muddy legs
Almost clotting the wounds
This transfusion is molesting my being into some malodorous monster,
the purest form of impurity
My claws weigh heavy on my finger tips
The serrated point of my growing tail slowly starts to slither across my
thigh
Accidentally pricking into it
Starting a small stream of blackened chunky blood to run down,
streaming through the ditches of scars dug into my knee
The breeze flows my cold tears backwards, away from my eyes
But freezing the veins it crosses
I scramble into a cave
For I feel the bubbling heat of springs inside
I nestle within, hugging my bruised knees
It's simply a place to hide
And here I lie, until the chilling frostbitten veil of winter is purged by the
sun...

DERELICTION

Iron oxide soaking out through my decaying skin
Sanguine stains across my chest and thighs in forms of verses
Holy verses
In which my skin burns at
A defect in the creation of man
Or at least that's what they say
Innocent in the start
But through the outré mutation
My soul turned black
My skin turned pale
For I've been hiding inside my happy place, where the prayers color the halls with sound
I've been stuck in a plastic skin
Syringes hanging from my veins
Wandering through the cold hallways of the church
I go into paroxysms
For every Nun and Priest stares at my sin
They're recondite to whom I may be
All they can see are the inverted crosses and horns
The pointed tail and the black nails
The drained sympathy has influenced me to lose my wings
I was almost human
Now I'm almost inhumane
Yet as I cry in the dusty antediluvian corner while the preacher cries his words to the children of God
I scribble all my confessions in my own blood
Yet they refuse to look as my screams echo across the halls
I crawl away
Slithering like the mere worm I am
And though I prayed to the holy incandescent cross hanging above
I was never answered, never healed
For I was left aside, scrapped
Hidden like a blemish across the walls of God's kingdom
And though I was remitted
The omniscient creator abandoned his creation
Left him to be tortured
Left him to decay under the towering figures of mankind
So the creation abandoned him..

DEVIATION

Faintly dazing through my mind where clockwork churns and cracked
bronze cogs grind
I open the butterfly covered doors that lead into this satire realm covered
in spider webs and mutilated reimagined dreams
I can see the blank porcelain faces of imaginary friends crack and break
apart
Exposing the malevolent being they truly are
They are an ink black effigy engrossing me, dancing in fantastical
strokes of liquid limbs
They entangle me in physical strings of awe
As they stab into my heart with serenades formed into hooks that then
drag me through a field of singing daisies and hooded figures chopping
away at the flower stems with scythes
Each figure looking into my soul and smiling widely at the sin it sees
Their eyes glowing red and their body's fading into sparkles and ash
I awake, poking my fingers through my skin
I'm trapped within myself
A dried husk of my former being
I crawl through the scab my fingers leave only to see waterfalls of pig
blood and hear screams of agony incarnate running at me with an
inhuman form of movement
Each arm dragging through the sticky blood covered ground
I back away and incidentally trip, noticing my legs are entangled by
snakes of gluttony, eating away at the flesh and gnawing on the bone
There I fall through a slimy floor of the blood
It stains my alabaster skin as the crimson melts to ink
The black liquid seems possessed as it floods into my stomach
Drying where I lay
My eyes scurry left to right
Up to down
As I stand
Throwing up gallons of shiny ink
I wobble through
Dripping a utter darkness that then forms together into words across the
ground
Syringes that move like frightened worms prick into my veins
Filling me with audacity
But it turns poisonous as I approach
The needles curl in my skin
The scene, horrific in nature, soaks my eyes in tears and blood
As the ghosts of my remains cover my peeling chunks of flesh with old
crumpled sentimental letters and cover my twitching eyes with sheer
cotton balls
They swim around me in smoldering spheres of euphoric senses pushing

me slowly off the edge and into a wine glass full of severed heads and cardinal tinted influence
There I fall and become engulfed in the morbid mixture of death & drunk suppression
Beneath the wrapping of love notes I smile, burping out bubbles within the glass
For I'm caught in the bliss of ignorance
Floating within it as everything around me turns to an abysmal state, collapsing in on itself
My mind is crumbling, the gears smashing to the floor
The imaginary walls melting down into pools
The ground cracking and breaking apart
Yet, as I drown in the wine glass, it all is meaningless to me
And my lungs burst, inevitably, like the breaking of my sanity, the tearing apart of my care, and the melancholy fading of my hope..

JEFFERSON

I moved here after I died

The people smiled day by day

The people cried night to night

The bookstore is run by a murderer

I saw the stars above the church laugh

The doctors use zippers instead of stiches

The patients moan in pleasure when they see him

They drive like idiots here

I had lunch at a local veggie shack but I smelled steak in the back

I hear military launch codes in the static of the radio sometimes

I hear gurgles in the bathroom of my hotel room at night

I saw all the elevators in town have a 13th floor

Everyone feels like cardboard sometimes

I saw an angel on my toilet

The stray cats stare at you here, that's all they ever do

There's a porn shop by the local church

Some old lady runs the place

One guy only speaks Latin

Everyone leaves at Halloween

My bed smells like dirt

I saw a tree with B heart S carved into it

Some guy hung himself from that tree

I noticed a month later it S heart B right under it

Some other guy killed himself under that tree in August

My calendar only has August in it

I woke up one day with a S drawn on some nametag stuck to my face

I eventually left

Their airport was beautiful

Their travelers were bleeding, dirty, and crying

One of the travelers had a noose hanging from his briefcase

The pilots had smoke rising from their mouths

There was a kid playing with his toes three seats away

He had no hair anywhere and only wore a hospital gown

Some old man was crying, his wrinkly face pressing against the window

They didn't serve us any nuts

Some old bald guy with no teeth was eating cashews, his gums bled but he didn't care

The pilot kept crying on about his wife over the com, suddenly talking in a bold professional tone

"Sorry about that folks" he confidently said

A train crashed into our plane

I moved here after I died

THE BROKEN LANTERN

My fists punch the hollow walls of the prison that is my poisoned mind. My tears they flood my soul. My eyes re-open to a new day of failed confession. I open my mouth to admit but the only thing that comes out is fear in a chilled fog. I concept ways to say what I fear, but the fears eat my tongue. Then I fall, I fall into a deep lost forgotten hole only to find a new hole to fall into. I try to re-open my eyes but my fear stitches them together forcing me to rip them open to yet a new hole I fall into, each with a new challenge following a new exit. I wonder if I will ever escape these caves. Then you came along holding a lantern, spreading new light into the dark void. When I got lost in the dark you would hold my hand giving me guidance and giving me light. Then you fell into a hole, thus breaking the lantern and breaking our grips. I yelled for you, only gaining silence, then I heard you, you said keep going so I did such. I found the exit and I found the color of life yet also losing the color of you. I cried, I mourned losing you. I miss you. I miss you forever and will never forget you. The stitching in my heart is from the hope you gave me. My mind purified and open from the light you opened to me. I love and miss you.....

BEREAVEMENT

Life held only by strings

Delicate strings

A truth within it

A vibration breaking it

Its stretch is shattering

A small sound echoes through the lonely abyss of death

Ripple upon ripple burst through the earth

As the dripping tears of souls in regret, sadness and madness shed upon the grave

These strings of life drift

As the remnants of memory fade

They are forgotten

The inevitable evaporation of essence dies out like pitiful embers fading in flame

The skeletal hands of death have put it out by a veil of cold darkness

No, he can't be gone forever, they scream!

They scream it to the crucified Jesus as they place every hope in an after life

The strands of life were forged into a noose hung from about,

Created by incandescent bullies

That has ended a life that only just begun

ENIGMA

Softly I gag as I cough up the animated arm of the one who holds my
mutilated soul
They squeeze it, dripping the acidic blood I contain into my eyes
Acidic from rebellion and confusion and the anxiety swimming within my
veins like a parasitic worm feeding itself
The blood melts through my already blinded vision
It exposes the twisted thoughts breaking through my skull, escaping
through my eyes, mutating my outlook
My muscles tighten
As hooks jam through my ears and raise me slowly I'm suddenly
surrounded by the societal demands and restrictions that eat away at my
confidence and feed my fears
The cold grasp of two hands carve it's nails into the middle of my face
It tears away
Tears away my identity
Time after time
Mask after mask is being ripped from me, exposing who I may really be
But there is no end
All that remains is the pain and blood left after each scratch and tear
All I am is a puppet controlled by fears and love, hatred and the euphoric
sensation of social acceptance
I try to close my eyes to fade from the truth
But my conscious corrodes, it burns pessimistic futures into the back of
my eyelids
It's all I see when I shut it all out
So I deafen myself with screams and blind my mind with the hypnotic pull
of televised imagery of society's standards for who I think I am
I stuff my stomach full of sugary treats to cure the incurable sickness that
floods my veins with emotions of self-hatred
And now I'm being dragged from the safety of solitude and into a dream
where my fantasies have turned into nightmares
I stitch my lips shut and blindly write
Shivering from the loneliness though I'm surrounded by many
It feels like this life is a fear inducing misadventure where every fantasy
has a morbid twist
It's ironic.. The years I should be living are the years I seem to be dying

EUTHANASIA

My veins swell up, violently pulsing up through my skin
As I melt through the dried breaking skin of reality
Shattering into a wall of hands
Each jamming their dirty palms into me grasping my breaths and tearing
out the air within
Suddenly chained down by rules of society
The element called 'me' is stripped from mind
The maggots of humanity, jammed into the cortex of my mentality, are
eating away at the personality hiding between the left and right sides
The recalibration has initialized
The contamination of my soul is spreading through each artery
Remember I'm inside this husk of manipulated love
The voices crawling through each ear bleed my mind, birthing migraines
Melted hands of mine wrap across, holding my skull together
Ink running down my arms, they show the finger prints of my poisoners
Fusions of venom circulate with each pulse of the dying heart held
behind these diseased bones
Breaking down what inside, my dead heart I throw up
Lubricated by blood and worms it lays there
I guess I'm dead inside..

DECAY

The screeching nightmares that shatter peace are distaining this so called "reality"

The soulless crowds watching as the ticking clock chimes

The bats inside rip themselves through the flesh barrier

Which lies in between

Such madness is ill inspiring

Shellshock to the inner locking chain of an insolent pretense

Desperate screams go silent

A noiseless horror has been seeded,

Color coated with self-righteous divinity

The Cheshire grins

Ripping apart while their mocking eyes gaze,

Staring though

Wake Up

Wake Up

Wake Up, they chant

As the syringe bobs with racing heart beats

Pointlessly, cries echo through the halls of the asylum

Wake Up

Wake Up

Wake Up, they chant

OSSEIN

Your body's decaying away

Silence

Blissful silence

The syringe keeps bobbing with heartbeats

A shiver in your spine

A quiver in your deathly ridden heart....

Just wake up

TRIBULATION

The cracked plague mask rests desolately upon the dusty stones

The populous destroyed, abandoned due to this Hell sent disease
The posies faintly dancing with the wind from the porcelain white mask's
beak
Stenches of decaying corpses and shit that's piled up along the
European alleyways taints the foggy air
Its so silent
So dead
Crows squatting to feast on the diseased flesh
"What have we done
Why do you punish us,
God?"
"Redemption" they scream
As the living tear off their cloths
Shaking each other out of anger and fear
"Whip me! Do it Brother, Do it Sister! Drive the leather and spike into my
flesh…! Into your flesh! God must know we repent!"
They scream it
The women smudge their blood into their eyes, they just want to be
cleansed
But they're filthy…
The children sing as their skin breaks out in black patches
"Ring around the rosy
Pockets full of posies
Ashes, ashes
We all fall down"
They let go, quickly being lunged backwards into their coffins
Still alive but they're really dead
Right?
This disease has surely killed them by now
Right?
Their tiny nails scratch as the dirt compiles on top
Their loud screeches fade as they slowly suffocate
As others are drug away by their hair, their mother and father stuff them
into this pile of corpses as the fire cleanses them of Beelzebub's curse,
of God's ailment
Flailing as their flesh falls off, melted; Ashes Ashes We All Fall Down
"Everyone's gone"

The little girl remarks as she looks for her Mother

Wake up Mommy

Wake up. Daddy said he's feeling ill
Her eyes roll back, as the skeletal hands of the reaper tears through her
eye sockets
Pulling the little girl into Mommy's mouth
Pulling her through Mommy's throat, stretching the trachea
Pulling her into darkness
The darkness of this plague
Into this Hellish shadow that veils upon Europe
The Lamb broke one of the seven seals
The Pale horse of the Fourth Horsemen gallops from Hades
Death
This must be the Last Judgment...
His scythe slicing through women and men
Child and Elder
Sending them to the depths of Earth
Mass hysteria, mass death
It coats this mortal plain
Everyone's dead

BEDLAM

Pressure inside veins
Piercing splinters carving through skin
Lights, they're fading fast
Suddenly, duct-taped bodies rise through steel floor
Upon the tape lay drawn on words
Harsh words
The bodies' heads twitch
Suddenly their wrist slit, rope rings across their neck
Holes form across their temples
Keyboards in their hands, phones, and webcams
The devices fall to the ground as the duct-taped bodies fade
Running away, Converse to cement echo through the narrow hallway
Past bleeding lockers
Searching for the blind teachers
They lean down but as they stare their faces go bleak
Faceless, blind and deaf to you
Nowhere to hide, the only sanctum is within the mind
Then their words form like fishhooks that jam into our once thought safe
imaginations
Insanity is creeping, squirming around under the eyes
Digging into the ears, the screams blow out eardrums
The red stains the floor, as the dread infects
Then rings the bell, it's vibrations bounce around your tears
One by one those tears drip upon your books
As blood runs onto the binder

COLORLESS, TRANSPARENT, ODORLESS

I am the fluctuating waves
The base entity for everything

My might is malady to humanity
As it is a vitality to all

For I am the fluctuating waves
An entity of mysterious misery
My liquid skin is a beautiful gleam that attracts the treasure seekers
Just as my small scaled creatures attract the idiotic child

I am the fluctuating waves
The galactic life giver
A universal creator to a heartbeat, your blood is thicker than my water for
my oceans gave rise to the connecting cells of your bloodstream
You are me
The fluctuating waves of the seas
My ethereal body has witnessed all, my oceanic embrace has been in
and out from your lungs
I have been the frosted tail to Haley's comet
And I have been the destroyer of cities
You can hear me in hollow shells
The soothing screams of the sea
The lullaby to love found among men and woman resting upon my soft
crusting
For I am the fluctuating waves

I am the rain and I am the untamed reckoning

The moon is the composer to my songs of liquid requiem
Listen to your mother's voice
Let the sound of my flowing body rest yours into the sand, let my serenity
wash you away to esquivalience and a delicious inertia
For I am the true umbra of earth
For I am the fluctuating waves

THE TOOLS AND THE TOYS FOR THE 5TH CARDINAL SIN

Bursting through the shadows with this silver thorn's glint
Like that of the frightened insect's fang

These lambs bleed, run
These fields turn cold, they deform into a gray

As the acute steel slowly slides in between the vein
The jugular

The heart of this virgin lamb's motionless husk of flesh and curly white hairs
It's crimson coating slips across the tip, dripping upon the cloud's face

This sleek simple element of molded shiny earth has become such an ailment to the masses
A distinct fear among those who've been scarred by it's beautiful body, by its blood curling shine
To both the innocent and the guilty, To the Evil and To the Holy

Molded into many forms, some to behead, some to burn, some to engrave, some to sacrifice
Some just to separate butter from it's mother-body

A mass of glistening chromium jutting into tendons, through muscles, accidently piercing into bone
Truly a mutant, a disgusting creation of man, they stole it 'her' from nature, from this planet's core

Yet beautifully deadly, the blinding precision of it, held in the right hands, insights adrenaline
Just for it to cut through

This platinum rimed bringer of silence feels nothing,
Repents nothing,
But is the catalyst for Everything

PLASTIC PAVEMENT, RUBBER SKIES, EARTH DIES

Converse on pavement
Head down to the quivering ants scurrying away
As the cold desolate gaze of night shines upon shining chains
Suddenly it all falls in, trees bend as road melts away
Reality kicks in as stars fall crashing into earth with simply broken strings attached
Grass floats away while fear breaks into the brain
Screams echo from across the broken neighborhood
All while the sun seems to fall away, appearing cardboard instead
Headphones bump around mid-air with the heavy beat
Nothing was as real as we thought, while Earth bounces around a child's room in disarray
We were all just a child's toy
Heat falls as a shivering cold emptiness joins in instead
Just as fast as it started it died, along with earth and the cruel creatures upon it

PROBLEMS BEHIND ZIPPERS

A boy in the dark

Zipped up silent

Only left alone in his mind with secrets

And the more he thinks about them the more the lies flood his vision

Tears start to run down his emotionless face

Hiding away behind lies

Guarded by a fearful state of mind

And calmed by fragments of truth that lay behind

Then as he wanders past his memories of confusion

He suddenly turns on the TV to make his mind stop the thoughts

And yet again the zipper stays zipped-up... Tight

But in the moments of this saddened state full of defiance and forced conception he wants to tell someone

But sadly he can never find the words to describe this feeling and truth

In this state everything goes black as words wander by like a cold wind

His pupils dilate as his heart gasps to see the truth like a beached fish near the ocean

But the water is always too salty and it always dies away in the end

Then as the moon comes up and his eyes close he always dreams the same thing

A false love full of inaccurate feelings covered by lies and smiles

Yet the true love is full of hate and disgust

A confused self-decision is his only known answer

And there is no going back after this choice

Hate and ignorance is the punishment for unzipping the zipper

But what lies under this zipper is his mind and soul

Joseph D. Brutto

SEA SHELL

Soaking within the sea
A mixture of seaweed and shit
I crawl out of this seashell I lay within
This filthy shell stained with moss and beheaded beetles
Their sticky yellow blood and organs squeeze out onto the gleaming
skeleton of snails that I've been nestled inside of
I arise like the dawn's sun that has painted the sand with orange
And as I break open my sand crusted lashes I stretch my fingers apart as
a embryotic slim from my oceanic revival reconnects my fingers back
together
It's dripping from my nose and rolling into bundles pooling at my barnacle
covered toes
I open my mouth to bring in the fresh salt stained air, only to have a lilli
pad grow from the back of my throat reaching up to the clouds
Aquatic vines tangle in between my cracking teeth flailing down my chin
and across my chest hugging the ridges of boney ribs
Butterflies dance across my coral crusted skin
Breaking the dried sand into grains falling at the slightest touch
My skin crawls from the water moving up through it
Inevitably compiling in my skull and out my sundried pupils
I smile
As my pale skin is warmed from the tropic's warm breeze
It was once cold within that shell
Cold and blue but out here it's alive and it's euphoric
The tulips rising from my shoulder's pores
Its so euphoric yet as I curl my fingers they shatter
Like a seashell
First my forearms and next my chest
My face and now my legs
I crumble to the floor
A broken seashell waiting to be washed out to the sea

STITCHED HEARTS

Empty prayers echo through lost minds
False love lasts a few hours longer
Dreams never last, broken minded souls fused together
Just trust in time to decide our life's fate
You and me, stitched hand in hand
Thoughts processed as the ticking from clocks melt into heads held high
Drugs in our system, **bludgeoning** the truth with this... strange that what we share is full of lies
Our hearts asleep as they walk into this double edged sword, piercing the fragile skin
Is it just a thoughtless dream filled with malice or... an unbelievable real thing?
Please do not wake this sobbing mind
I will not hear goodbye
I will not have 'No' stain this loyal heart
Are you still there?
Do my cries echo, heard by nothing, in the dark divines?
Must I kill a man to prove I am not another thing you seem to play with?
I try... I try so hard to lie to myself
This is not love... or is it?
I am drowning in a jet-black sea of stress
I do not want to be a forgotten puzzle piece to your life
Coughing up blood as my mind is shot
Why won't you go away?
I hate you...
This rain plummeting to the pavement
It reminds me that our hearts lay within one of those drops of water
Fragile but so pretty
Falling to a pointless end
Feeding a flower, growing into something bigger
My pens have been dry, for you are the devotion to all my time
Just a word from your tongue bursts my heart into happiness
Just a word from your hate bursts my heart into pieces...what are we?
My stomach has been eating my heart lately
And my love, this writing really empties me
I feel drained inside
I wonder if you'll ever read this
I love you...
But I hate you...

Joseph D. Brutto

THE DARK ONES

As dusk turns to nightfall

After the moon covers dawn all the souls sleep

The dark ones come out to play

They crawl through the cracks in the windows

Squirm beneath the door ways and stalk down the chimneys

Melting down, they crawl into the children's nose

Break into, then, corrupt their souls

Their reach crawls through the delicate child veins

Neither a pop nor a tear, just a stealthy movement into the bloodline

They start to feed off envy and kick start puberty

These children act like prepubescent teens

Stolen whisky and empty flasks decorate the house

At first this was a beautiful generation, full of hope and glee

Now it is a waste of creation and filled with idiocy

Welcome children to our lovely twenty-fourteen!

THE DOOR IN THE DARK

Sitting in the dark as fears form puddles around him
The torture of silence and seclusion, his only friend is the teddy bear he holds so tight that he was to give to his love as a gift
As the rats tap across the dark steel floor, his echoed sounds of grief swim through the lightless prison
His nails scratch slowly across the floor as he stares at a door in front of him
His small arm reaches out a little to the door handle and as his little fingers almost grasps it, he stops
A thought passes through his scared mind..."what if it is worse on the other side?"
He puts his arm down and wraps it around the teddy bear then scoots back into a corner
He wipes away his running sorrows and rubs his wet baby blue eyes as he starts to sing sad love songs to himself
His halo is duck taped together, but still broken like his ego, will and smile
The torture of the dark silence is nothing compared to the fact that he will never see love....Just that damned door that gloats and depresses him
His freedom is his imagination and its tales of impossible futures keeps him sane in the dark
Days pass as his gaze does not move from the door
Inevitably the curiosity gets the best of him
He gets up and crawls to that door
Suddenly ink melts from its sides so he backs away
A prayer to every God of every religion pours from his shaking lips as his heart pumps from fear
His palm turns the knob as he holds his teddy bear as tight as he can

WICKED TRANSFUSION

Dripping down my chin, black ink
My tears are mixed in
I am crawling on my knees, leaving a dotted trail between
Hate flies past my grieving body, cutting through inch by inch
It is flying at my face
Suddenly it breaks and materializes as a chain, wrapped like a noose across my throat, piercing into my brain
I am pulled up into the sky
Finally, after agony it drops me free but I fall into a sea of tears, blood and dark dreams
Gasping for thin air I reach towards the surface as the blood sea fills itself into me
Bursting through my stomach it drowns me from within
Cracks spawn across my skin while skeletons are pulling me beneath
I scream
The last time I may ever see such clarity
The blood sea it burns my gaze
Pupils dilate as I am pulled through the ashy red sea
Knives run up my ribs as a chorus of souls shout that these are curses and tricks
This is deadly irony for this is just my heart killing me
My eyes turn white stripped of color and sight
I wake up in my bed covered in cold sweat shouting AMEN
These Hebrew words don't seem to work at protecting me from the nightmares in my life
Nor the monsters under my bed for their claws reach for me
There goes my sanity
I swear these monsters are just kids
Their segregation is tearing me up from within
My angels are gone
Demon's dawn
Maybe it is just a new beginning, but wait... kindness must come back for me
I refuse to be what made me
I refuse to contort into such an inhuman thing
A monster of a Saint
Maybe a demon in the wake
There goes my purity
There goes my morality

Be silent as she thinks, deep down, how's it make you feel to know you're not dead yet? That's right, shut up. Shut up and speak already. Good God, you're more silent than God himself. Bite into the apple of Eden, that pineapple shaped grenade. How's it taste? Like dust you say? Ugh no wonder you're in therapy. Please don't touch the merchandise. Hey! I don't care if you wanted love or not it's definitely not free if you want it you idiot. And here I was wondering what the hell your saying, could you please maybe talk? Like about your problems? Problem? Get out then, it's not fair. It just isn't: Now get out! Fucking tourists.

Just my random thoughts

Joseph D. Brutto

THE THIRD BREATH OF A CORPSE

Cherry stems weaving through my skin, lacing in between every disc in
my broken spine
Honey suckles cramming down my throat
I collapse into this black ethereal beach
My nail less fingers pull a hollow body
Just a dying rose, a paramour parched for sunlight
But these vines I call veins are used to the hypothetical famish
Want to walk a mile in these decrepit shoes, these painted converse?
Well I'm either crawling or running
I'm always running. . .
This body is numb
Inure to it all
But this mind isn't, the fat juicy seed of electricity can't cope
Deep within the core, past the truth of the lies and within my secrets are
where the faithless slits dwell
They try to fix it, but their fingers are too fat to stitch it all up
I fuck myself one moan at a time
Just like everybody else
But you don't look at me like anybody else
And to me your just another awkward glance, maybe just a Like, maybe
just another picture on the wall that my lighter hadn't kissed yet
They draw harsh things into my skin, labeling the body
But I'm Joseph. . .
Joseph
Joseph
Joseph
Joseph
It means something about God you know.
God
They say, "Only God can judge you child"
But in that case I'm fucked
I'm lost within this preverbal bleeding session, an inertia flowing through
my stomach
The stomach that ate this heart
I need a transplant, a flashback on how to breathe
Because these lungs seem filled heavy with malice and screams
I can't swallow so he forces it down
Cum, blood, and divinity
I keep having tremors in the dirty water of this chilled steel tub
I thought it would clean me
It just burns
My bones are breaking
From the weight of nothingness
I screamed when he found me

I screamed when they found me
Are these delusions?
I cried when he lost me
I cried when they abandoned me
My toes curl up in the black sand and my eyes dilate when the sanguine
touched my hips
Cherry stems tie in circles around my identification
Continued from the base of my spine
There's no blood drying my flesh, just ash growing and breaking down
from the cancer I ate
I wanted to call the ending a requiem
But, no one ever showed up, so I couldn't. . .

HUMAN FLESH TASTES LIKE PORK

Child, lay down tonight
Let the satin sheets purge your blight
Silence, let them give you delight
It's a faint sin
But just let the toxin sink in
Enjoy the sensation running across your spine
Please, drink the wine
Devour the supple fruit, ignore the fly
Break apart the bread, please don't cry
Just lay down child
Don't let your mind become riled
Rather indulge in the eyes of the reviled
They devoted their body to this meal
Of course I'll never allow it to reveal
And the chefs, their mouths have literally been sealed
So just rest my child
Enjoy the juicy flesh of the vile

ONE TRICK PONY

He suckles on the wine's grapevine
A simple intoxication
Breaking the oath of fidelity
A recent heresy
As this skin has broken
His last recantation
His teeth won't let go of it
A supple taste oozing upon the liar's tongue
We've drawn a line neither may pass
But these children cross it like a tightrope
We've learnt the rules, and we scream like newborn titans of a giant's
womb
Reciting them, the echoing of his past
He sleeps, his mother's voice on the other end of the cord
A movie burnt into the left halve of his brain
A love song etched into the other
We painted him every day
In every way he was our little boy
a recreation of what we did to ourselves
But we didn't do anything for him
Except change what he was born to be
Inside our arms we embrace a whisper
A hated truth we all accept with denial
We haven't seen her in a while
They shoveled the darkness upon her
And I
Well I held her down
The fear beckoning from her eyes
She's 3 feet under,
a list of why we should dig her up
is stapled on the refrigerator
And she suckled on the wine's grapevine
Breaking the oath of fidelity
Her teeth wouldn't let go of it
A recent heresy
In the midst of February

A CAPTAINS HAT AND GOD'S SURCOAT

Breathing into my skin
A shattered hasp merged across my lips
And roses distorting my vision
A deepened hand reaches into my stomach
Slipping through the skin
A captain's hat
And God's black fringed surcoat rests on my shoulders
Along with faces of the lost
Ethereal bodies of a subliminal kind
They called me creative
But it's just an expansive vocabulary and a ting of luck
All these words rotate in rows across my body
White and red letters
Black highlights decorating the moving screens of A B C's
A glamour in the fleshed out ink
A book filled with inaccurate sensations
Don't stop staring
Look a little closer
In the past, always beneath the skin
Because within I'm a mystery
Dried out lips and melting eyeliner
The hand sleeping inside my soul
Snaps and strums the arteries
I fall straight back, my mouth filling with a film
A childhood recorded in a cold setup
I hold on to the time passing by
My palms numb, fingers slipping
My body drowning as this frail realm tears
An etched out malice in the sky of a lost subconscious
Etched out in my skull
The carvings of my own personal Hell
And my first sin lies in the middle
The mistake of meeting you
The second plunges my memory through a process of deteriorations
It was straying
Watched constantly
And these sections of history seem to repeat
A cringed ruffle and bleached blood oozing across paper
The destructive forces my fingers create were the third
Fire, blood, sticks and fucking stones
But you know I love the pain
"You've changed" they softly said
And I nodded slowly
Because my personality is split

There's Shawn, and some malformed manifestation of Joshua to just
name two
Their patterns marked with the slits on the wall
Covered by the portrait of a killer
Black chalk and a vellum sheet
First the eyes, so he can see its soul
Now the arms, so it can hold itself together
Next the head, so it has something to hang
Nothing else
It's incomplete for a reason
Just look through the remnants of the mirror
Tangled hairs
Frisked virility
Hidden under dirty electric guitar riffs
A deafening beat
And the screams of a relatable man
A figure of masculinity that never stayed
A gun to our temples
And a captains hat on our head
They whisper to stay quiet because were not done
I melt into the cobwebs
Beneath the delicate spider silk
Underneath it all lay pictures of suffering and pumpkins grinning
An intimacy shared with each sleeping soul
A closeness only a razor could reach
But not against my wrist
No, against hers
A taste of tap water and pennies
It fills their lunges
I could only sit and read
Because those red and white A B C's were all that were there
Highlighted black and stabbing into my body
She was almost dead
He was seconds from breathing the sea
He didn't think he was good enough, in short he wanted to drown it away
And they were only two out of dozens
I see them as reflections
History
I think of them when I can't swallow my tongue
Suicidal tendencies
I know the sensation
Of murder and self-infliction
It's only been 17 years and I have seen, heard, read, experienced more
pain than this worldly body can contain
And they call it 'creativity'
Stuff it in a book filled with false sensations

Joseph D. Brutto

Call it 'poetry'
I know how this all will end
A pretense I can't help but to deny

PERFEKT

He's resting in a jar on a shelf
But it was only yesterday he laid against that tree
Filming the world with his magnificent eyes
Their sparkle almost gleaming through the camera
Little pigments now possess his body
The one resting in a jar on a shelf
Deep inside each fragment is a new little dimension to him
A different aspect of his memorial being
In this one here you can see how he roars
A bandana wrapped across his blue hair
And across his palm it reads 'perfekt'
A deviation of the word 'perfect'
As I'm sure you caught on to
And in this one you can see him being held back by chain, like a lion
His hair spiking out like a mane
And his gaze penetrating your soul with a ferocious stare
Why are my tears so thick when I see him during his primed lion's roar?
When I witness him smile. . .
Love. . .
Live. . .
When I see him laugh. . .
And I can suppose I'm crying because he's gone
And is resting in a jar on that shelf
I haven't even met this lion held back by chains yet
But mere chains can't hold back someone like him
What makes them think death can?
Where am I going with this?
Is this a poem or a monologue?
I thought this was about him being perfekt. . .
Because that's what he is; perfekt. . .
And I can only meet him while he rests in a jar on a shelf, in the confine
of my soul, in the moments I feel alone, when I don't know what to do,
when I dream, and maybe if the scriptures actually are true then in an
afterlife
It is what I ask myself in other words "What would he do?"
But until then, I can only talk to my role-model through an imaginary
realm where I've displaced my soul

FATHER IN HEAVEN

I seem to be crawling into
 broken screams of a babel
Cold voices of lost men
Touching me venially through the crowd
As I move ever closer
Drifting into this sin of hubris
A despair filling this inconsistent sunset
These eternal sands embrace us
And we writhe
Waiting for our train
A prescription
We pray through our seven dialed goggles
But the preacher man just fucks us
Under God's eyes
And they sing
Doctor Jamie and Madam Bell
A hymn in June
pointless to a sinner
And these confused men still touch us
An imprint from each supple fingertip
Across our waists
A tally of sin
Leaving us mutilated
Leaving us abused
But we're still pure
To you
God
Father in heaven
But our faith sways
And you left
You left
And you left
Us to our misery
You left
God
Father in heaven
Us to be molested
Reprobated
Unworthy
And you left
God
Father in heaven
We bite the hand that feeds
We were clearly diseased

A filthy child, fatherless
Motherless
For our mother was a virgin
And our father was a teacher of lies
Because we bite the hand that feeds
Hungry for more than an unholy taste
Snip the black lamb
And break the 7th seal
Again
And again
Leach death from our fears
And feed us when we fade to limbo
We craved indulgences
Because you left
God
Mother in heaven
Father in bed
You left
My God
My Inducer
My father
In bed
Why have you left?
They lit these wicker statuettes
Ancient trinity's effigy
And she cried the last rites
She repents the dogma
An oracle to our torture
But she has disembodied the physical realm
Mother in heaven
Father in bed
Why have you left us?

ABOUT THE AUTHOR

Joseph Brutto is seventeen years old and raised for the most part in Louisiana where he resides with his mother and older brother Cole.

Joseph had his first work published at the age of ten and since then has been published multiple times for his poems and prose since 2012 when life events created this writing outlet for him.

Readers will find his work to be very emotional, self-enlightening, a little dark, but also very deep and raw. Joseph has peeled back several layers of himself in the creation of this collection of poetry.

www.ingramcontent.com/pod-product-compliance
Lightning Source LLC
Chambersburg PA
CBHW070025110426
42741CB00034B/2564